Thirty-One Prayers for my Wife

SEEING GOD MOVE IN HER HEART

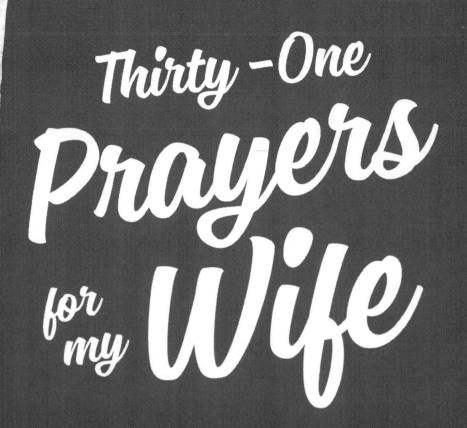

D0030054

Aaron & Jennifer Smith

A HUSBAND REVOLUTION RESOURCE

Thirty-One Prayers For My Wife

Seeing God Move In Her Heart

Written By Aaron & Jennifer Smith

Copyright © 2015
Smith Family Resources, Inc.

ISBN: 0986366714
ISBN 13: 978-0-9863667-1-0
LCCN: 2015910635

Book Website
husbandrevolution.com/31prayersbook

Printed in U.S.A

CONTENTS

SEEING GOD MOVE
Psalm 107:28-30

"Then they cried out to The Lord in their trouble,
and He brought them out of their distress.
He stilled the storm to a whisper;
the waves of the sea were hushed.
They were glad when it grew calm,
and He guided them to their desired haven."

INTRODUCTION

Marriage is a powerful reflection of God's love story. A husband and wife reflect the covenant relationship of Jesus Christ and His bride, the church. We are the church! Jesus patiently pursues each one of us. He has an intense desire to have an intimate relationship with us, regardless of our sin, faults, and failures. His love truly is unconditional and perfect.

As a husband I am commanded to love my wife just as Christ loves the church. I didn't fully understand the magnitude of this call on my life as a husband when I first got married. I loved my wife, but I didn't know how to love her unconditionally. There were things about her that irritated me, there were moments I felt so disrespected by her that I harbored anger in my heart toward her, and when the greatest struggle we faced lasted almost four years I was ready to give up on our marriage completely. Although it was difficult to love my wife unconditionally, I continued praying for her and for our marriage. Even when she refused to pray, I prayed for her. God was pressing into my heart the significance of praying for my wife and my marriage. Day after day, no matter what happened, I prayed.

God heard me and He transformed everything. I saw God move in my wife's heart!

Praying was way more powerful than trying to get my wife to do what I wanted her to do or to be the wife I wanted her to be. Desiring things to change in our relationship and knowing I didn't have the power to fix everything all the time, I submitted to the Lord. I asked Him to help me, to change me, to inspire my wife in a profound way, and to heal our brokenness in our marriage. My wife and I began growing in our relationships with God. I started to understand my role as the leader of our home, a husband who cherishes his wife and a man who needs to walk in integrity. My wife began to grasp the importance of her role as a wife and the influence she has in our marriage. Together we received wisdom regarding God's purpose and design for marriage. Growing closer to God radically transformed us.

Prayer has revolutionized my relationship with God and with my wife. I wrote these thirty-one prayers with my wife's help, to encourage you to pray for specific areas of your wife's life. I urge you to use these prayers as a guide, but also include your own desires and hopes for your wife and marriage! Each day's topic may not apply perfectly to your wife's circumstances, but you can still use it to guide you as you add to each one your wife's needs. I believe these prayers will spark a passion in your heart to trust God, to lean on Him and to experience more in your relationship with Him and with your wife.

Submit your heart to God in prayer and you will see Him move in your wife's heart as well as in your own heart. You can read straight from the text, you can say these prayers out loud, you can get on your knees, or you can stand with your arms raised up toward the sky. You can assume any posture you desire, there is no right or wrong way to pray. Just do it.

This is not a magical book that has any guarantee that your wife will change or that you will change once you reach day thirty-one. If you do not notice any change, do not be disappointed or discouraged. Praying for your wife and your marriage requires faith, to believe even before you actually "see." It is imperative that you do not look to this book as a means to fix your wife or your marriage, but that above all else you trust in God wholeheartedly from now until forever. The goal of this book is to give you the courage to pray continually with and for your wife. My hope and prayer is that you would continue to pray each and every day.

I hope these prayers remind you to pray for your wife and

your marriage in specific ways. May you be blessed as you step into The Lord's throne room and petition for one of the most important relationships you have been gifted.

I have included a few challenges to encourage you to think about the importance of prayer in your marriage. There are a total of 7 challenges for you to consider. I urge you to pray about each one and fulfill it when and how the Lord leads you!

If anything from this book inspires you to update social media, tag me @husbandrevolution and #HR31Prayers so I can follow along and see what really stood out to you in this book!

Dear Heavenly Father,

I pray for the husband holding this book right now. I ask that You would anoint him as he commits to praying for his wife. Please inspire his heart to make each prayer his own by adding his wife's specific needs to every one. Give him the courage to do all the challenges in this book. May Your Holy Spirit lead him as he leads his wife in prayer. Bless this husband and his wife. Move in mighty ways in their lives. I pray Your will be done in their marriage.

In Jesus' name AMEN!

HELPER OF THE HOME
EPHESIANS 5:23

DEAR LORD,

Thank You for my wife. Thank You for considering every detail of her life and everything about her that makes her different from me. I appreciate her emotions, I value her opinions, I love her body and I am grateful for her heart. You have equipped her with unique talents so that she is able to fulfill Your will for her life, one of which is her role of being a helper. I pray my wife sees how significant her role is of being a helper in our marriage. Give her understanding in this area of her life and give her encouragement to do all that You desire, with a heart of joy. I pray You would reveal to my wife all the ways she can be a helper to me and a helper of the home. May Your Holy Spirit walk with her throughout the day, showing her how to manage her time effectively so that she is not stressed out. I pray my wife grasps that being a helper is not about making me happy or having a perfectly clean home, but it means coming alongside me spiritually through prayer, emotionally through affirmation, physically through intimacy and mentally through positive communication. Help her to see the influence she has in my life. May You bless her for her obedience and give her strength to continue on even when it is hard.

In Jesus' name AMEN!

PERSONALIZE:

Use this area to write a personalized prayer for your wife. You can also write a list of things you would like to continue to pray for.

MY WIFE'S WORK WEEK
Colossians 3:23-24

DEAR LORD,

Thank You for all the abilities You have gifted to my wife. She amazes me with how much she is capable of handling. Her mind is sharp and her body is strong to be able to work as much as she does. May You open her eyes so that she sees her value in all the abilities You have given to her. I pray that You give her endurance this week. If ever she feels faint, tired or drained, may Your Holy Spirit anoint her with relief and comfort. Help her to feel rested and give her time to be able to take breaks from her work so that she is rejuvenated. Help me to step in and encourage her with words of affirmation and appreciation so that she knows what she does is valuable. I pray no matter how busy her work week is, she is able to persevere with cheerfulness knowing confidently that she is serving and honoring You. Please fill her heart with patience for those who are near her while she works. Lord, give my wife a desire to share with me about her day and all that she did. Help me to be a good listener. My hope is that we never allow our work to define how we treat each other. Help both of us to communicate any frustrations that stem from work, but then let go of them so that they do not cripple our intimacy.

In Jesus' name AMEN!

PERSONALIZE:

Use this area to write a personalized prayer for your wife. You can also write a list of things you would like to continue to pray for.

ENCOURAGEMENT FOR TODAY
Romans 15:13

DEAR LORD,

Thank You for today. Thank You for my life and my beautiful wife. She is the best gift I have ever received. I pray my wife overflows with hopefulness today. I pray she earnestly seeks intimate time with You, reading Your Word and praying. My hope is that she reads a portion of scripture that speaks into her life. May she sense Your presence close to her and may You reveal to her precious truths about who she is and what her future holds. Holy Spirit teach her Your ways and use me to lead her in those ways. I pray my wife is also encouraged by other women today through smiles, hugs, words of appreciation and recognition. Use people to show her just how much she is loved and cared for. Use me to lift her up, to affirm her, to thank her, to bless her and to connect with the deep places in her heart. I pray and hope our marriage is an encouragement to her as well. Lord, I pray she is content with our marriage, yet hopeful for the maturity we both will continue to experience as time goes on. I pray joy is evident on her face, through her eyes and through her every smile. Remind her that she is worthy and that You love her so much. Overwhelm my wife's heart with peace by the power of the Holy Spirit.

In Jesus' name AMEN!

MATURING MY WIFE

Ephesians 4:14-15

DEAR HEAVENLY FATHER,

Thank You for Your loving-kindness. Thank You for my best friend, my wife, who loves me with the same kind of love that You have for me. Your example of true love has transformed us and our marriage in extraordinary ways. We continue to mature individually and together as one. We are nowhere near being perfect, yet love seems to cover all those imperfections we have so that we can still experience intimacy. There are times that my wife and I struggle with conflict, but we also reconcile through the power of grace and the willingness to apologize and forgive. Thank You for giving me a wife that knows grace. I am confident that regardless of our disagreements or moments of selfishness, our marriage will continue to grow deeper and more intimate. God, guide her heart through Your Word and help her to submit to You in prayer on a regular basis. Mature her understanding of who You are and may Your relationship with her grow exponentially. I pray against the enemy and any deceitful people the enemy uses to tear us down. Bind the enemy in Jesus' name and protect my wife from being tossed back and forth by any kind of teaching or trend that is not of You.

In Jesus' name AMEN!

Challenge

Start a journal. Write down what God is teaching you as well as a prayer. Be sure to include a specific prayer for your wife. Journaling sounds daunting, at least for me it does, but it doesn't have to be anything huge. Just right out some things you want to pray for and write down what you will be reading in the Word that day. Don't over think it.

FREEDOM FROM FEAR

Philippians 4:6-7

DEAR LORD,

I love my wife so much. I desire the best for her. I pray that she would feel secure in our relationship and secure in my arms. I do not like seeing my wife suffer from fears or worry. I pray I can be a strong support for her during those times, reminding her that You are near. My prayer is that she does not consume herself with anxious thoughts, but rather dwells on the promises in Your Word. May Your Holy Spirit help her to surrender her fears at the foot of Your throne. May You free her from any negative thoughts that attack her heart and mind. May You pour out your peace over her, that it may run over her body. I pray my wife would trust me to lead her. I also pray she trusts You to lead her. May she find her security in You and may You increase her faith. Free my wife from fear and worry. Use me to comfort my wife and point her always back to You. If there is anything pressing against her, anything stirring stress in her life, anything that triggers worry, I pray against it in Jesus' name. Strengthen my wife and keep her joy in tact, for without joy our marriage suffers. Help both of us to discuss our worries and lift them up in prayer instead so that we do not react out of fear and hurt each other in the process.

In Jesus' name AMEN!

MY WIFE'S HEALTH
3 John 1:2

DEAR LORD,

Life is fragile. My wife is fragile. This does not mean that she is not capable or strong, it simply means that she is delicate and that life is fleeting. Please help me to remember this daily so that I am motivated to take advantage of our time together to love and love well. I pray a blessing over my wife's health. I pray she remains physically strong, mentally sound, emotionally stable and spiritually submissive to You Lord. Continue to refine my wife and mature her with wisdom. Her well-being is important to me. I pray that I can help her stay healthy by making decisions that support good health. May we operate as one, willing to encourage each other in every aspect of our lives. My desire is for her to live a happy life, free of sickness or injury. I realize diet and preventative care both play great big roles in maintaining her health, so I beg you to motivate my wife to pursue a healthy lifestyle. Help her to eat right, exercise, and get adequate rest. If she refuses to make healthy choices for her body, please convict her heart on the matter and help her to change. I pray that if my wife is currently or in the future experiences pain and suffering, please heal her completely.

In Jesus' name AMEN!

EXERCISING SELF-CONTROL
Proverbs 25:28

DEAR LORD,

I pray my wife has an incredible day, full of laughter and love. May You do something personal for her that reminds her that her life has purpose. I pray I can be a source of joy for her. I pray my wife is diligent to succeed today in the plans she has made in her heart that are aligned with Your will. If there is a moment of temptation for her, I pray she exercises self-control. Open her ears to hear Your voice leading her to freedom and away from sin. Remind her to walk in the Spirit. Empower her to resist temptation and resist the enemy. I know she can overcome as she relies on You, Father. In any circumstance that may confront my wife today, may she have the strength to surrender the desires of her flesh and instead faithfully choose to react based on what You have taught her. When she is with others I pray she has self-control with her words, using them to edify others not tear them down. Help her not to gossip or slander. I also pray she has self-control with her eating habits, what she chooses to listen to and what she does when no one is watching. I pray my wife walks with integrity. May she be patient and think through every step that she takes today.

In Jesus' name Amen!

Challenge

Ask your wife to write down a list of specific prayer requests she has and refer to that list during the week as you pray for her. You can also add them to your journal for a quick reference!

GRACE IN MARRIAGE
Hebrews 12:15

DEAR LORD,

Thank You for the gift of marriage. My wife is my intimate lover. Being one with my wife has taught me so much about my relationship with You. Thank You for the purpose of marriage and how You designed it to reflect Your love story through Christ. I pray that I can love and lead my wife, just as Christ loves and leads His Bride, the Church! One thing I have learned from Christ exemplifying what kind of husband I am called to be is the power of your amazing grace and extending grace in marriage. I pray my wife and I are always humble to extend grace to each other. I pray no root of bitterness would ever find a place in my wife's heart against me. If there is ever an issue between us, please help her to communicate clearly with me and me with her. I pray my wife would feel safe to come to me and explain how she feels. Give me ears to hear her without wanting to get defensive. I also pray my wife is quick to listen as well and slow to become angry. Help my wife to live in an understanding way with me. Help her to apologize and forgive with a humble heart so that intimacy in our marriage can thrive. Lord, help my wife, and I gift each other extraordinary love through the power of your amazing grace.

In Jesus' name AMEN!

CLING TO THE TRUTH

Ephesians 4:2-3

DEAR HEAVENLY FATHER,

I pray for my wife today. I pray you would inspire her heart to be creative in the way that she expresses her love for me. I pray Your Holy Spirit would guide her to soften her heart towards me in a vulnerable way. Help me to see when she is being vulnerable and to remember that she is delicate. I have a responsibility to love and cherish my wife and I desire to do that, I just need help knowing how to do that, especially in those vulnerable moments. Holy Spirit help me to respond in gentleness and cultivate a desire in my wife's heart to want to be gentle towards me. May her body language, tone, physical actions and everything that she does, honor me as her husband. I pray she respects me as her husband. I pray everything she does accentuates the femininity in God's design of her as my wife. I pray that my wife only clings to the truth. I pray against the temptation to misinterpret what I have done or said as meaning I don't love her. Make her so secure in You that she does not have to wrestle with any insecure thoughts about my love for her. I also pray that she is quick to make every effort she can to keep the unity of the Spirit through the bond of peace in our marriage.

In Jesus' name AMEN!

CONFIDENCE
HEBREWS 10:35-36

DEAR GOD,

I am grateful for the life You have gifted to my wife and me. My heart is full of appreciation for all that You have provided for us and the hope You have filled us with. I know it is because of You that my wife and I are married. I have confidence that You are the glue that holds us together. I pray my wife would have an increase in confidence. I pray she never battles with thoughts of doubt, fear or insecurity. May You increase her faith and remind her why living out each moment of the day in faith is so important. I pray I can support my wife's faith in You by leading her to You. Help me to pray with her and to read Your Word together with her. May You give my wife courage to face hard seasons in life and courage to love well. I pray against the enemy's schemes to get my wife to doubt how much she is loved or valued. Build her up with encouragement from me and others today. Lead her through scripture impressing on her verses that will contribute to growth of confidence and courage. Please help my wife to stand strong, to persevere, and to do your will. May she be a woman of confidence who fears only You.

In Jesus' name AMEN!

FORGIVING MY WIFE'S SIN

Matthew 6:14-15

DEAR LORD,

Thank You for my wife. It has been beautiful to witness her grow and mature in You and in our relationship. I know she struggles with sin, but You know every detail of how and why she struggles. I pray You would intercede for her and help her not to sin. When temptations come her way, may Your Holy Spirit direct her decisions. Equip her to resist and say no! Open her eyes to how sin affects her, as well as how her sin affects the quality of our marriage. Please remind me to pray for my wife daily, especially over her battle with sin. Don't let her believe the lie that she is alone and please don't let her isolate herself because of shame or guilt. I pray that my wife is able to share with me what she struggles with. I also pray that she has a heart of repentance when she sins. Help me to forgive my wife's sin and give me eyes to see that she is in need of transformation that only You can provide. Lord, help me overcome any hurt and pain caused by my wife's sin and please help me to stop sinning against her. I implore Your Holy Spirit to teach us the deep meaning of forgiveness and the power it has to reconcile and heal any brokenness in our relationship we cause because of sin.

In Jesus' name AMEN!

Challenge

LEAD YOUR WIFE BY INVITING HER TO PRAY WITH YOU IN THE MORNING.
HOLD HER HANDS WHILE YOU PRAY OUT LOUD.

LIFE GIVING WORDS
PROVERBS 18:21

DEAR LORD,

Being married is such a blessing to my life. I love my wife with all of my heart. May You inspire me to show my wife just how much I love her in new and meaningful ways. Lord, I thank You for my wife and all the detail You poured into creating her. I specifically lift up the words she chooses to use and the ways in which she says them. Your Word says that life and death are in the power of the tongue. We know this very well. I pray she understands how significant her words are. May Your Holy Spirit reveal the impact her words make. May she choose to always use life giving words that edify and encourage. Refine her speech and refine her delivery. I pray her words always reflect the respect she has for me in her heart and I pray that she uses her words to affirm me in my role as a husband. I also pray that she never fears initiating in conversation with me. Give her the courage to open up her heart and be vulnerable with me. Please help me to listen and respond to her with life giving words as well. Help me to satisfy her desire to emotionally connect through conversation. May my wife know Your Word and may she share it with me to remind both of us of Your truth, especially in tough times.

In Jesus' name AMEN!

CULTIVATING ROMANCE

Song of Solomon 1:2

DEAR HEAVENLY FATHER,

I know that romance is a significant part of marriage. However, when life gets overwhelmingly busy, when we are tired or when we get used to our daily routine, it feels challenging to cultivate romance. I pray You would inspire my wife and me in different ways to meet each other's need for romance. Help us both to have the energy to initiate physical intimacy. Holy Spirit remind us throughout the day to think about each other, to consider how we can lavish our love on one another. Please press upon our hearts the urgency of spending quality time with each other every day that we are given, because we are not guaranteed tomorrow. Stoke a passionate desire in my heart to intimately pursue my wife. I pray her desire for me increases too. Lord, please provide the time and resources for us to date each other for the rest of our lives. Whether we have to schedule it, be flexible or spontaneous, I pray my wife and I would do everything in our power to make romance a priority. I pray that we would kiss and hug more often. I pray my wife would feel loved by me and to confidently know that she is the only one for me. I pray for a marriage full of romance, not lacking in anything.

In Jesus' name Amen!

KNOWING HER PURPOSE
ROMANS 8:28

DEAR LORD,

Marriage is an incredible mystery. I love exploring it together with my wife. We experience the ups and downs of different emotions felt as we live together in this covenant of marriage. Our relationship has encountered both good times and hard times, joyful moments and painful moments. Yet, all of it helps us understand Your great love all the more! I pray my wife knows her purpose in life and in our marriage. Reveal to her the woman and wife You created her to be. She is worthy, she is able, she is exceptional. I want her to be confident in who she is and what she is capable of when she trusts in You. Give her supernatural confidence and a faith that never fades. I pray she finds her identity in You. I pray she embraces Your will for her life. Open her ears so that she can hear Your voice and all that You ask of her. Satisfy her longing to belong, to feel wanted, to have meaningful friendships, and her longing to matter. Holy Spirit please remove any ounce of complaint from my wife so that she does not miss out on fulfilling her purpose. I implore you Lord, to guard my wife's life and defend her against the enemy as she seeks to love You and do your will.

In Jesus' name AMEN!

LOVE
1 Corinthians 13:4-8

DEAR FATHER,

Thank You for defining what love is. Your Word is clear about how I can love my wife and how she can love me. My heart's desire is that we love each other according to Your Word. I pray a blessing over my wife and ask that You anoint her with the ability to love me like You love. I pray she is patient with me. Help me not to stress her out or be a burden to her. Help me not to frustrate her in any way and if I do, help her to extend grace. May kindness be a strong quality she possesses. I pray she is never overcome with jealousy. Remove any arrogance or pride from her heart. Holy Spirit motivate her to act in a way that is honorable and respectful. I pray my wife does not just take from our marriage in a selfish way, but gives generously to sew love into our relationship. Help her not to be provoked easily. I pray she does not hang on to my past sins or ways that I hurt her. May she truly forgive. Lord, fill her with hope for our marriage so she remains secure. May my wife's countenance and composure reflect the character of Christ. Continue to mould her into the loving wife You created her to be. May the love we have for each other inspire other married couples to love as You have defined for us.

In Jesus' name AMEN!

Challenge

INTERRUPT YOUR WIFE WITH A ROMANTIC GESTURE WHILE SHE IS IN THE KITCHEN OR PICKING UP THE HOUSE. INVITE HER TO DANCE WITH YOU OR GIVE HER A COMPLIMENT OR TAKE THE MOMENT TO PRAY THAT HER DAY GOES WELL.

GAINING MORE WISDOM

JAMES 1:5

DEAR LORD,

Thank you for revealing great truths to my wife. I pray she continues to learn and grow in her relationship with You. May You bless her with Your wisdom. Fill her with knowledge and deep understanding. I pray she would be able to retain all that You share with her. Help her to fully comprehend Your Word as she spends time reading scripture. I also pray that she comes to me with any questions or doubts so that I can lead her to Your truth. I desire to contribute to her growth. Please equip me to be able to lead her in faithfulness. With the wisdom she gains, may Your Holy Spirit help her apply it daily. I pray she is able to put into action all the truth You share with her. God, I ask that You would continue to give wisdom to my wife generously, that she would know and do right in every situation. I pray the wisdom you give her positively impacts our marriage, building my trust in her, and ultimately increasing our intimacy. If my wife feels as though she lacks wisdom, I pray she would call out to You, Lord, and ask for it. May the wisdom we gain bear fruit in our lives as we implement what we are learning. May we never stop growing together with You and with each other.

In Jesus' name AMEN!

PROTECTING OUR MARRIAGE

2 THESSALONIANS 3:3

DEAR LORD,

There are times that I get frustrated by my wife and I allow my negative feelings to dictate how I respond to her. I am so sorry for doing this. Please help me to be kind to my wife. I pray that both of us can respect each other. I know that the enemy is real and that he will tempt me to do things that are unloving toward my wife. Please help me stay strong and resist the enemy. I also pray my wife does not give in to temptation to sin against me. Help both of us to put on the armor of God and fight as a team against the enemy and his evil ways. I implore you to protect our marriage. Strengthen the areas of our relationship that are weak, the parts that are vulnerable to attack or temptation. I pray that my wife and I can build up our marriage together every single day. I humbly pray for my wife today. May You encourage her and comfort her. I ask that You would provide for her in any area of her life that she has a need. Remind her that You are there for her and that You will never forsake her. Thank You for Your faithfulness, Lord! I ask that You bless our marriage. Guard us against the flaming arrows of the evil one. May your Holy Spirit remind us daily to intentionally invest into our marriage.

In Jesus' name AMEN!

MY WIFE'S NEEDS

Philippians 4:19

DEAR LORD,

It can be so easy for me to get my feelings hurt if my needs are not met by my wife. I apologize for being so selfish and I repent of being so self-focused. We both have needs and we both need to mindful of how we can fulfill each other's needs. Open both of our eyes to see each other's needs and motivate our hearts to action. I pray my wife's needs are completely met according to Your will. I pray I am a husband who seeks to serve my wife. I pray her need to be cherished by me is filled today. I pray her need to feel wanted by me is filled today. I pray her need to know that I see her as beautiful is filled today. Holy Spirit equip and empower me to fill my wife's needs today. Any needs she has that I am not capable of filling, may You graciously meet them for her. Lord, I ask that we experience a time of intimate connection today. I know my wife's soul is replenished when we take time to be together, when we chat about our day and when we embrace with physical touch. I pray all those things happen today. I pray against my flesh and any attitude I may have that would hinder any of that from happening. It would bless me to hear my wife express how content she is in life and in our marriage.

In Jesus' name AMEN!

A SERVANT'S HEART
Matt 20:25-28

DEAR HEAVENLY FATHER,

Thank you for sending Your Son to save the world! There are no words to describe the joy in my heart to know that Christ came to save me and to save my wife. Jesus Christ is my example for how I am suppose to love my wife. I pray I can be the leader and the lover You created me to be, You call me to be. I pray that my wife and I can serve each other daily. Not because we are slaves to one another, but because we love one another and desire to yield our hearts in humility to one another. I pray my wife is willing to be the wife You call her to be. I pray she would have a desire to serve others, including me, with great joy. Fill her heart with passion to go the extra mile, to love without conditions, to radically impact lives through generosity. Holy Spirit enable my wife and I to serve others together. Show us another couple or a family in need and then help us to bless them. I desire to serve in Your Kingdom alongside my wife as a team. I receive so much joy from being one with my wife. I love seeing us work together as a team. It is incredible how marriage is a reflection of the Gospel. Lord, may You be glorified through us and through our marriage.

In Jesus' name AMEN!

LIGHT IN A DARK WORLD

Ephesians 5:8

DEAR LORD,

This world is dark. This world is full of sin. Every single day the darkness collides with my marriage and tries to tear it down. There have been times that my wife or I have let the darkness into our marriage contributing to ugly conflict. However, You have called us to live as children of light. I want to shine brightly in this dark world as victors for Your name's sake. I desire others who are lost in the darkness to find You! May the light that shines from our marriage by the way we interact with each other guide others to You, Lord. I pray my wife chooses to live in Your light and not in the darkness. Give her eyes to see how the enemy tries to secretly ruin what we have. I pray she would choose to resist the enemy and resist temptations to sin. Push aside everything that tries to entangle us. Lord, I am confident that you joined us together as one flesh to do great things in Your name. May You open our eyes and impress upon our hearts the desires you have for our marriage. Holy Spirit guide us as we choose to follow you every day. My heart's desire is that we both, as Your handiwork, fulfill the extraordinary plans You have prepared for us and our marriage.

In Jesus' name AMEN!

Challenge

Ask your wife if you can pray for her. Gently lay your hands on her wherever you feel comfortable and begin by asking the Holy Spirit to lead you. Then take a few moments, uninterrupted, to pray for your wife.

MAKING GOOD CHOICES

Proverbs 16:3

DEAR HEAVENLY FATHER,

Thank You for my beautiful wife. Thank You for bringing us together and maturing us along this journey of marriage. I am learning about the great responsibility I have in leading my wife. You designed marriage with order and I realize that order is a good thing. As I lead my wife I pray for wisdom to make good choices. I pray my wife and I would choose righteousness. Holy Spirit permeate my wife's heart and mind. Help her to make wise decisions as she goes about her day. Remind her of the repercussions of sinful behavior, but also remind her of the benefit and blessing of making good choices. No matter where she is or what she is doing, I pray my wife submits herself to You. I pray she commits her plans to You and allows room in her day for You to lead her no matter how that changes her plans. God, please move in her heart, speak to her, guide her. Help her to remain pure and holy. Every decision she makes has a ripple effect in our marriage and I desire that she understands the weight of that. Establish my wife where You desire her to be. Plant gladness in her heart. May she be content, happy, excited for the future, loving and wise.

In Jesus' name AMEN!

DISCERNEMENT
PSALM 119:125

DEAR LORD,

I pray for my wife today. I pray she intentionally makes time to read Your Word and pray. Give her a hunger and a thirst for Your Word. Give her a craving in her soul to know You more intimately and send encouragement throughout her day to remind her to keep her eyes on You. May each and every verse she reads speak volumes to her. God, I pray she would be secure in her identity found in You. I pray she would know her value and find confidence in You alone. Protect my wife from the ways of this world and from the temptation to doubt Your love. Gift my wife discernment so that when she reads Your Holy Word, she understands it. Use me to help her answer questions about faith and marriage. Use me to set an example for my wife in how often I read the Bible and pray. I believe having discernment is vital. It is the gift of judging well, the ability to know right from wrong. In our marriage alone it is important for her to be able to judge a circumstance and choose wisely what to do about it. I desire her to be a woman after Your own heart! Thank You for my wife and thank You for pursuing her. I pray she reciprocates Your love and joins Your invitation to live out an extraordinary life full of joy.

In Jesus' name AMEN!

PROTECT HER HEART & MIND

ROMANS 12:2

DEAR LORD,

Thank You for my wife and the way that she loves me. I am so grateful for the life we share. God, I pray protection over my wife's heart and mind. I know You created her with a variety of different emotions, but I pray she does not let those emotions lead her. I pray she would rely on You and Your truth to lead her. I also pray that she would not let any insecurities she may have affect her today. Eradicate insecurities from my wife's heart and mind! I pray against the temptation to dwell on the negative in her life. May every step that she takes today be taken in faith, courage and confidence. I pray every ounce of her being is strengthened. Protect my wife from believing the lies of the enemy. Protect her from assuming the worst about me or others. Protect her from people who seek to take advantage of her or who seek to hurt her. Be her defender! Help her not to conform to the patterns of this world. Whether she is exposed to something deceiving online, on television, from her friends or family, may she stand strong in faith, without wavering. Renew her mind and replace any negative thoughts with Your Word of truth. In all she does, may she glorify You and honor our marriage.

In Jesus' name AMEN!

INITIATING SEXUAL INTIMACY
HEBREWS 13:4

DEAR LORD,

I pray for my marriage right now. I pray specifically that sexual intimacy between my wife and I would improve. Help me to romantically pursue my wife and become so familiar with her likes and dislikes that I am able to please her. I also pray my wife takes time to know me and become familiar with my likes and dislikes. I pray this area of our marriage would always remain a priority to both of us. Help me to connect with my wife on an emotional level throughout the day that would cultivate a desire for sex. I desire to make her feel wanted and truly loved. I pray my wife views sex as a gift from You. May she understand how it blesses both of us and deepens our bond with one another. I pray she is willing to initiate sexual intimacy and that she finds joy in being with me in such a vulnerable way. Please help me to make sex romantic and fulfilling for her. Lord, I pray a blessing over this aspect of our marriage. Please be our shield to defend sexual intimacy from everything that threatens to keep us separated. I pray my wife would have an insatiable desire for me. I pray I would also have an insatiable desire for her. Help us to honor our relationship and help us to keep our marriage bed pure.

In Jesus name AMEN!

Challenge

Lead your wife in a prayer asking God how you and your wife could bless a family in need. Then at some time during the day do what you both feel led to do for that family.

FILL HER WITH COMPASSION

1 Peter 3:8

DEAR HEAVENLY FATHER,

I love my wife and I feel so blessed to be able to share this life with her. Please fill my wife with compassion, the deep, awe-inspiring compassion that makes up the heart of Jesus. My wife already cares deeply for me and for others, but I pray that she is filled with unconditional love for all. Yet, provide her with structure and boundaries so that no one takes advantage of her or our marriage. I pray her life leads people to You! May she be sympathetic to the sufferings of others and may You equip her to fulfill their needs. I pray those whom she helps would never see her compassion as a desire to form any type of relationship that would compromise her vows of marriage. I also pray that my wife would have a sympathetic attitude toward me. I ask that we can be in a constant state of understanding one another and extending grace to one another. I pray my wife would be compassionate with me, especially when I am having a rough day. I pray our intimacy increases as we love and serve one another. God, please bless our intimacy and help us to connect in a deeper way. May Your Holy Spirit anoint my wife and use her to do great and mighty things for You.

In Jesus' name AMEN!

MENTOR YOUNGER WIVES

Titus 2:3-5

DEAR GOD,

My wife is amazing! She has blessed my life in so many ways. My desire is that she honors You in her role as a wife. I pray she lives a Holy life in submission to You out of reverence. I pray You would transform my wife in any area where she is in need. Develop a strong character in her and increase her faith, so that she will be able to teach and mentor younger wives. The rising generations need You, Lord. They need great examples of what a marriage is like, they need to know marriage was created with purpose and they need to know how to fulfill the roles You intended for them. The sanctity of marriage is threatened by the ways of this world. The need for strong men and women to teach what is right and what is good is obvious. I pray my wife builds relationships with other wives and I pray she inspires them to turn their hearts to You. May she affirm them and may she teach them how to love their husbands. Use me as well! I pray I can build strong friendships with other husbands and inspire them to love their wives. Relationships are so valuable. Open our eyes to see the value in others around us. Show us how our marriage can be a blessing to teach others Your ways and Your will.

In Jesus' name AMEN!

REJUVENATE MY WIFE
Psalm 23:1-4

DEAR GOD,

I pray for my wife right now. She endures throughout the day, from morning until night. I pray that You would give me eyes to truly see just how much she contributes to the quality of life we have, please give me a heart that genuinely and deeply appreciates her, and give me words to sincerely show my thankfulness to her. Anoint my wife with energy to get through her day. I pray she physically feels great today and I pray she is mentally sharp and focused. Help her to control her emotions. Allow her to feel deeply, but also process appropriately through Your perspective in any situation she encounters. Bless my wife by giving her rest as she submits her day to You. Lead her to a place of solitude. Rejuvenate my wife in a way that revives her soul. Lord, I ask that my wife would not be dismayed or overwhelmed by any circumstances. May she know You as her God and may she intentionally draw close to You. If she feels at all unworthy or unloved, I pray You would pour out Your peace over her. Reinforce in her heart and mind how valuable she is and equip her to carry out the purpose You have for her. Refresh my wife and refresh our marriage.

In Jesus' name AMEN!

BREAKING STRONGHOLDS
1 Corinthians 15:57

DEAR GOD,

My heart is overwhelmed. My wife is a good woman, yet there are many things she struggles with. Fear, anxiety, insecurity. Sometimes she struggles with having pride, sometimes she disrespects me, sometimes she acts irrationally and sometimes she loses hope in You and in me. This breaks my heart. I desire my wife to have a good life. I want her to be free of fear and worry. I want her to be set free from pride and doubt. I pray for freedom in her life from the strongholds that hold her down, bind her up, tear her to pieces and leave her feeling broken. I want my wife to be whole! I pray, in Jesus' name, that my wife be set free! God, I implore You to protect my wife from these strongholds that tempt her. Fill her with confidence and cover her with Your incredible peace. Strengthen her mind and what she believes. Strengthen her heart. I claim freedom from specific sin she struggles with. May she walk in victory! I have faith that extraordinary things happen when prayer is made a priority. Give me the courage to pray with my wife on a daily basis, especially over the strongholds that try to destroy our marriage. Help my wife and me to truly believe we are set free.

In Jesus' name AMEN!

GOODBYE PRIDE

Proverbs 11:2

DEAR LORD,

When pride come so does disgrace. Pride rooted in the heart is evident through body language and word choice. It destroys marriage and any other intimate relationship. I specifically pray against pride in our marriage. Having a prideful posture leads to self-preservation instead of protecting us as one. Help both of us to respond and react to each other with kindness and compassion. I pray You would strip my wife and me of pride. Help us to resist the urge to be right in our opinions and ways. I pray humility would be rooted in our hearts, so much so that there is no room for the seed of pride to be sown. Holy Spirit, I lift up my wife to You and ask that You would transform this area of her life. Reveal to her the truth that our relationship will always be more important than being right and more important than treating me with disrespect. My wife is a great woman and I know she fears You, I know she desires to have a character that reflects Your character. Please open her eyes and reveal to her any parts of her heart that are full of pride. Help her to say goodbye to pride, repenting of it and moving forward renewed in her mind and heart. Fill her with a desire to be a peace seeker and an ambassador for unity.

In Jesus' name AMEN!

INTEGRITY
Proverbs 10:9

DEAR GOD,

Thank you for my wife. Thank you for joining us together as one. I pray we grow closer together and experience deeper intimacy as we let down our walls, allowing us get to truly know one another. I pray my wife understands the value of integrity. I pray each and every day she lives her life with integrity. Holy Spirit, speak to her heart on the things she needs to repent of. I pray against any urge she may have to lie, make excuses, defend herself for actions that are not honorable, or justify any behavior that is contrary to Your Word. I pray against any behavior that is unbecoming or sinful. May she walk in Your ways and may her life be rich in righteousness. Lord, please speak to my wife and teach her what is right. I pray her heart would be full of desire to do what is right, whether or not anyone is around. Press upon her heart how to be an honest wife. I pray she is an encouragement to other wives to have integrity, to live with purity, to stand firm in faithfulness. Lord, please transform my wife and me so that we live according to Your will for us. I pray protection over our marriage and any temptation to keep things hidden from one another. May love abound in our marriage and overflow from our hearts.

In Jesus' name AMEN!

Challenge

Spend time praying with your wife right before engaging in sexual intimacy. Pray that God blesses your time together.

EXTRAORDINARY MARRIAGE

Mark 10:6-9

DEAR HEAVENLY FATHER,

Thank you for hearing my prayers and thank you for moving in our marriage. I am so blessed to have my wife, my lover, my friend. Regardless of any conflict we face, any trials and challenges, my marriage is a gift from You, a gift I embrace every day. Mature us and refine us so that we can help each other through this life together. I also pray protection against the schemes of the enemy, who seeks to destroy what You have created. May You bind the enemy in Jesus' name! Holy Spirit cover us and anoint our marriage. Break any strongholds in our lives and break our heart for what breaks Yours. Let compassion rule in our hearts! God, I ask that my wife and I would experience an extraordinary marriage. I pray our intimacy thrives, our communication is clear, our companionship a priority, and our relationship a reflection of Your incredible love story. As we are united and joined as one flesh, may our hearts yearn to keep the sanctity of our vows a motivator in our every response to each other. I pray You would move in my wife's heart and help me to see how You are moving in our marriage. I submit to You, Lord! I submit my marriage to You as well. May Your will be done in us and through us.

In Jesus' name AMEN!

A LETTER FROM
THE AUTHOR

DEAR FRIEND,

I commend you for diligently praying through this book, for putting your wife's needs above your own and petitioning for her before God. Do not let this be the last time you pick up this book and use the prayers to guide you. This is your resource and one that my wife and I hope you will continue to pray daily for your wife throughout your journey of marriage. I would love to hear all about what you experienced as you prayed for your wife! If you want, you can submit a post to social media, tag me @husbandrevolution (Twitter: @husbandrevo) and share so that I can see and other husbands can be encouraged! Be sure to also add #31HRPrayers so that we can all follow the conversations as other husbands around the world participate in praying these prayers!

DRAW CLOSER TO GOD & YOUR WIFE

GRAB A COPY OF MY NEW DEVOTIONAL, "HUSBAND AFTER GOD."

HUSBANDAFTERGOD.COM

HUSBAND
AFTER
GOD

Drawing Closer To God & Your Wife

Aaron & Jennifer Smith

A HUSBAND REVOLUTION RESOURCE

THIRTY-ONE PRAYERS FOR YOU

GET A COPY OF THE COMPANION PRAYER BOOK FOR YOUR WIFE.

SHOP.HUSBANDREVOLUTION.COM

Thirty-One
Prayers
for my Husband

SEEING GOD MOVE
IN HIS HEART

JENNIFER SMITH

An Unveiled Wife Resource

Get The Husband Revolution Devotional:

HusbandAfterGod.com

For more marriage resources please visit:

Shop.HusbandRevolution.com

Receive daily marriage prayers via email:

husbandrevolution.com/daily-marriage-prayer/

Get connected:

Facebook.com/husbandrevolution

Instagram.com/husbandrevolution

Twitter.com/husbandrevo